The Set-Up

Take the Plunge

Learn the 7 Habits®

- Use colored pencils or markers to highlight parts you want to remember.
- Memorize quotes.
- Study the workbook and think through the questions and concepts.
- Make the learning fun.

Live the 7 Habits

- Personalize and apply each habit in your life.
- Challenge yourself to move out of your comfort zone.
- Commit to do the baby steps at the end of each chapter in the book.

Share the 7 Habits

- Discuss with a friend, parent, guardian, or teacher ideas that are important to you.
- Share with someone you feel close to the commitments or ways you want to change.

To get the most from *The 7 Habits of Highly Effective Teens*, you have to make an investment. It will require time and commitment. Take a few minutes and glance through both the book and this workbook. Look at the pictures and read the headlines and quotes that interest you. Begin to get an idea of what this book is all about and what you might "get" from reading it.

Once you've glanced through the pages of the book and workbook, write your *personal expectations*—what you hope to learn—in the box below.

PERSONAL EXPECTATIONS

From reading *The 7 Habits of Highly Effective Teens*, I hope to be able to:

_____

_____

_____

_____

_____

_____

Get in the Habit

THEY MAKE YOU OR BREAK YOU

Habit 1: **Be Proactive®**
Take responsibility for your life.

Habit 2: **Begin with the End in Mind®**
Define your mission and goals in life.

Habit 3: **Put First Things First®**
Prioritize, and do the most important things first.

Habit 4: **Think Win-Win®**
Have an everyone-can-win attitude.

Habit 5: **Seek First to Understand, Then to Be Understood®**
Listen to people sincerely.

Habit 6: **Synergize®**
Work together to achieve more.

Habit 7: **Sharpen the Saw®**
Renew yourself regularly.

Now think the opposite way. Write an opposite statement for each habit. Come up with your own defective definitions. (If you need help, refer to p. 7.*)

Habit 1: ————————————————————————————

Habit 2: ————————————————————————————

Habit 3: ————————————————————————————

Habit 4: ————————————————————————————

Habit 5: ————————————————————————————

Habit 6: ————————————————————————————

Habit 7: ————————————————————————————

* All page references are to *The 7 Habits of Highly Effective Teens* book.

Paradigms
and **Principles**

W H A T   Y O U   S E E   I S   W H A T   Y O U   G E T

What is a paradigm? (para-dime)

A paradigm is the way you think about and see things.

Write your own paradigm about the kind of music you like best. Favorite type of music: Your views about it:	Find out what others think about this type of music. See how many different opinions you can find. Parent: Teacher: Friend: Other:

Did your paradigm change after listening to the paradigms of others? Why or why not?

_____
_____
_____
_____
_____
_____

What You See Is What You Get

"Paradigms are like glasses. When you have incomplete paradigms about your-self or life in general, it's like wearing glasses with the wrong prescription."

—Sean Covey

Take a look at the picture on this page. What does it look like to you?

This is a picture of: _____

What helped you come to this conclusion?

_____
_____
_____
_____
_____
_____
_____

What You See Is What You Get

Here's a more complete look at the picture from the previous page.

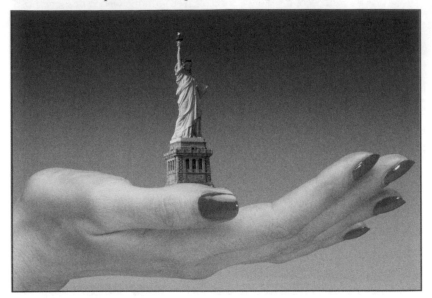

Is the picture what you thought it was? If not, you just experienced a paradigm shift—the way you saw something, your point of view, changed.

Some of our paradigms are about life in general. You can usually tell what your paradigms are by asking yourself, "What is my life centered on?"

In the outer circle, write the things that you tend to spend most of your time on (i.e., friends, school, church, music).

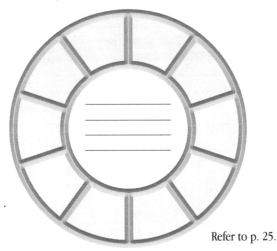

Refer to p. 25.

What You See Is What You Get

"The long and short of it is principles rule."
—Sean Covey

What is a principle?

A principle is a natural law or basic truth (i.e., honesty, service, love).

List other important principles:	Why are these principles important to you?
_____	
_____	_____
_____	_____
_____	_____
_____	_____
_____	_____
_____	_____

Which of the principles you listed are the most difficult for you to live?

In the center of the circle on the previous page, write in the word "principles." Below that list a few principles that you find most difficult to live. Decide what you will do this week to practice living in harmony with your most difficult principle.

Remember: Place principles in the center of your life.

PART II

The Private Victory™

Starting with the Man in the Mirror

> "If you haven't forgiven yourself something,
> how can you forgive others?"
> —Dolores Huerta

Private Victory: Self-mastery; winning the battles within yourself.

The first three habits deal with the Private Victory. Name them below.

Habit 1: _____

Habit 2: _____

Habit 3: _____

What have you done lately to exercise self-discipline (i.e., exercising, waking up on time, studying, controlling temper)? Draw or write your answer in the box below.

To get a clear picture of your Personal Bank Account, review the deposits and withdrawals you make during a week. Suppose each deposit you make is worth $1 to $100; however, withdrawals cost from $50 to $200. You determine how much you should deposit or deduct. Keep track of your total, using the form on the next page, and see how much you can deposit in a week (make as few withdrawals as possible).

The Personal Bank Account

Starting with the Man in the Mirror

Description of Deposit/Withdrawal	-	+	Balance
Stood up for something I believe		$75	$75
Read a book just for fun		$25	$100
Accepted myself as I am		$100	$200
Gossiped about a friend	$75		$125
Week Total	$75	$200	$125

Description of Deposit/Withdrawal	-	+	Balance
Week Total			

Make copies of the above form to help you keep track of your Personal Bank Account the rest of the week.

Refer to p. 35.

I Am the Force

> "Our only freedom is the freedom
> to discipline ourselves."
> —Bernard Baruch

What does proactive mean?

> Being proactive is the opposite of being reactive. It means to take responsibility for your actions.

So what does reactive mean?

> Reactive means to be acted upon and controlled by events and emotions.

When and where do you tend to be the most *reactive*? _____

_____

Give an example of a *proactive* choice you've made:

_____

_____

Below are various examples of reactive and proactive language. With two different colored markers, determine which phrases are which by highlighting *proactive language* in one color and *reactive language* in another.

"It's not my fault!"   "I will do that right now!"   **"I just can't decide!"**

"That's unfair!"   "I didn't see it that way, thanks for letting me know."   "If only . . ."

"Who does he think he is anyway?"   "Can we talk about this first?"   **"I'm sorry, I didn't mean that."**

"Leave me alone, you jerk. It's none of your business!"

Listen to your own language. Is it proactive or reactive? List some examples.

_____

_____

_____

Refer to p. 51.

Habit 1: Be Proactive

I Am the Force

Here are a few ways to apply Habit 1 in your life. Go for it, take the plunge.

* Do some of the baby steps at the end of each chapter in the book, starting with p. 28.

* Keep a journal/notebook.

* This workbook contains Notes pages so you can capture your feelings, thoughts, and ideas as you read through *The 7 Habits of Highly Effective Teens* book. Also use them to jot down insights that come to you as you complete this workbook.

* Over the next week, keep track of your language, actions, and choices in your journal or on a Notes page. Write down both the good and poor choices and actions you make on a day-to-day basis.

* Evaluate yourself each day by asking:
  —Am I being proactive or reactive?
  —Did I make good choices today?
  —Did I blame someone else?
  —What language did I use?

In the box below, give an example of one of your choices. What did you learn from it?

Habit 2: Begin with the End in Mind

Control Your Own Destiny or Someone Else Will

Habit 2: Begin with the End in Mind allows you to live your life with hope and a purpose.

"Think about your own life. Do you have an end in mind?
Do you have a clear picture of what you want to be one
year from now? Five years from now? Or are you clueless?"
—Sean Covey

Control Your Own Destiny or Someone Else Will

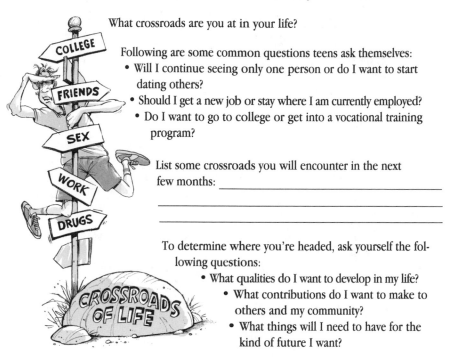

What crossroads are you at in your life?

Following are some common questions teens ask themselves:
- Will I continue seeing only one person or do I want to start dating others?
- Should I get a new job or stay where I am currently employed?
- Do I want to go to college or get into a vocational training program?

List some crossroads you will encounter in the next few months: _____

_____

_____

To determine where you're headed, ask yourself the following questions:
- What qualities do I want to develop in my life?
- What contributions do I want to make to others and my community?
- What things will I need to have for the kind of future I want?

To begin with the end in mind, you must know where you want to go, who you want to be, and what you want to achieve in life. So why not put it in writing?

Personal Mission Statement:

> A personal credo or motto that states what your life is about.

Why would a personal mission statement be important to you? _____

_____

_____

_____

_____

_____

_____

To help clarify what you want your mission to be, complete The Great Discovery activity on the next few pages.

The Great Discovery™

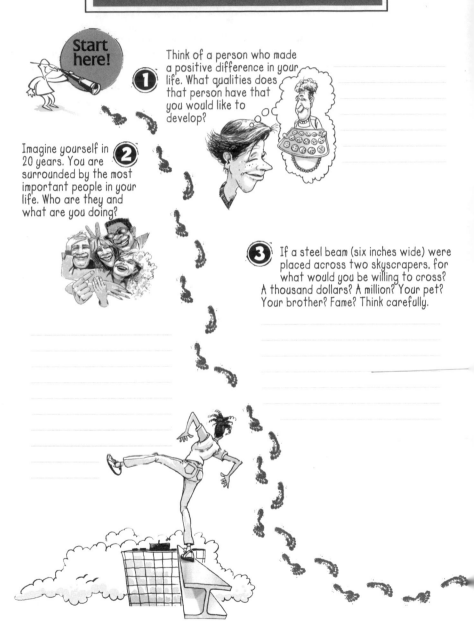

Start here!

1 Think of a person who made a positive difference in your life. What qualities does that person have that you would like to develop?

2 Imagine yourself in 20 years. You are surrounded by the most important people in your life. Who are they and what are you doing?

3 If a steel beam (six inches wide) were placed across two skyscrapers, for what would you be willing to cross? A thousand dollars? A million? Your pet? Your brother? Fame? Think carefully.

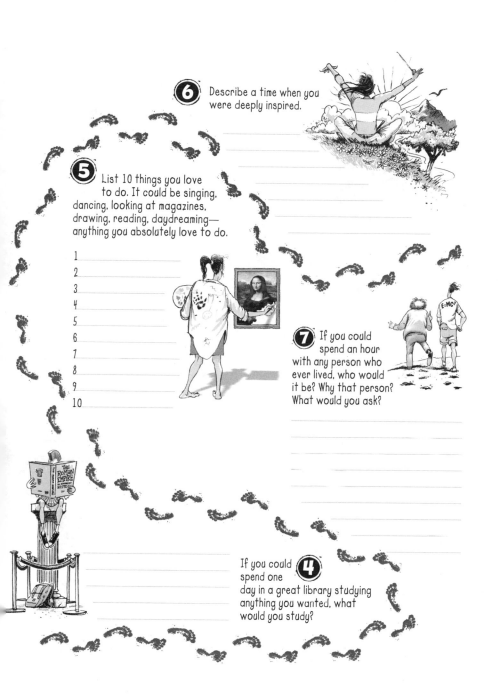

6 Describe a time when you were deeply inspired.

_____

_____

_____

_____

_____

5 List 10 things you love to do. It could be singing, dancing, looking at magazines, drawing, reading, daydreaming— anything you absolutely love to do.

1 _____
2 _____
3 _____
4 _____
5 _____
6 _____
7 _____
8 _____
9 _____
10 _____

7 If you could spend an hour with any person who ever lived, who would it be? Why that person? What would you ask?

_____

_____

_____

_____

_____

_____

If you could **4** spend one day in a great library studying anything you wanted, what would you study?

_____

_____

_____

_____

_____

17

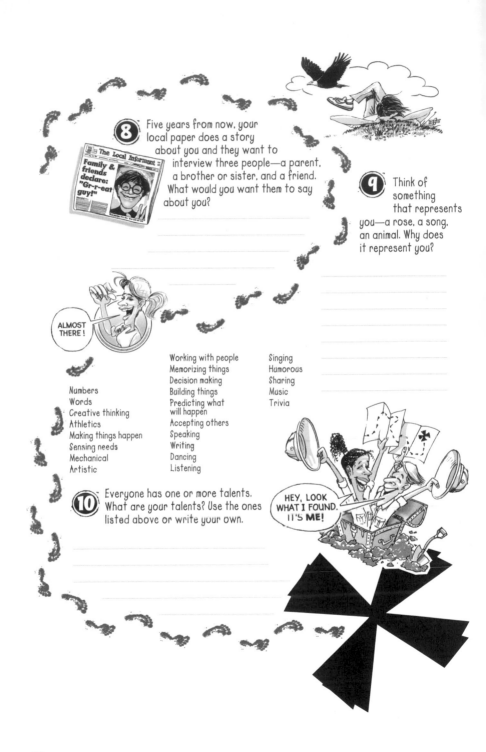

8 Five years from now, your local paper does a story about you and they want to interview three people—a parent, a brother or sister, and a friend. What would you want them to say about you?

The Local Informant
Family & friends declare: "Gr-r-eat guy!"

_____
_____
_____

9 Think of something that represents you—a rose, a song, an animal. Why does it represent you?

ALMOST THERE!

Numbers
Words
Creative thinking
Athletics
Making things happen
Sensing needs
Mechanical
Artistic

Working with people
Memorizing things
Decision making
Building things
Predicting what will happen
Accepting others
Speaking
Writing
Dancing
Listening

Singing
Humorous
Sharing
Music
Trivia

10 Everyone has one or more talents. What are your talents? Use the ones listed above or write your own.

HEY, LOOK WHAT I FOUND. IT'S ME!

Find pictures in magazines, posters, or personal photos that show the kind of person you would like to become and the qualities you value most. Paste the pictures below to help spark more ideas about your personal mission statement.

Habit 2: Begin with the End in Mind

Control Your Own Destiny or Someone Else Will

Review what you wrote in The Great Discovery and look at the pictures you chose to represent you. Now, make a list of the most important things you want your personal mission statement to include.

- _____
- _____
- _____
- _____
- _____
- _____
- _____
- _____
- _____
- _____

Personal Mission Statement Writing Exercise
Review the above list and the pictures and answers on the previous pages, then set five minutes on the clock and write all of the ideas that come to your mind during those five minutes. Go! Write fast!

_____
_____
_____
_____
_____
_____
_____
_____
_____
_____
_____
_____
_____
_____
_____
_____
_____
_____
_____

Control Your Own Destiny or Someone Else Will

Don't worry if your mission statement is not perfect at first. Work on it over the next few weeks—add more ideas if you want. Develop your mission statement until it is something you are proud of. Once you've got it, put it where you can read it often.

Refer to pp. 81–82 and 91.

Habit 2 Notes

Will and Won't Power

> "Things which matter most must never be at
> the mercy of things which matter least."
> —Johann Wolfgang von Goethe

Habit 3 Put First Things First: The strength to say yes to your most important things and no to less important things.

"Acting in the face of fear"

Give examples of the activities of each type of time manager.

Quadrant 1: The Procrastinator

_____

_____

Quadrant 2: The Prioritizer

_____

_____

Quadrant 3: The Yes Man

_____

_____

Quadrant 4: The Slacker

_____

_____

Refer to p. 107.

Habit 3: Put First Things First

Will and Won't Power

Time Activity

Where do you spend your time? On the lines below, write down how you spent your time yesterday. What took up most of your time? School? Work? Homework? Watching TV? Reading? Computer games? Hanging out?

Did the things that filled up your day matter most to you? ———————————

Where did you waste time? ———————————————

Where were you the most productive? ———————————————

Label each square of the time quadrants with the name of the time manager (procrastinator, prioritizer, yes man, slacker).

Time Quadrants™

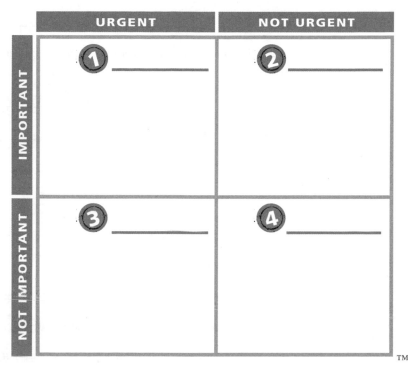

Review the previous page to see how you spent your time yesterday. Write each activity in the corresponding quadrant.

How many activities were focused on Quadrant 2? Write down other Quadrant 2 activities that would have helped you put first things first. _____

_____

_____

_____

_____

_____

_____

Refer to p. 112.

Habit 3: Put First Things First

Will and Won't Power

As you answer the following questions, think about how often you are in your courage zone.

- Think of a time when you acted in the face of fear and took a risk to move outside of your comfort zone. What did you learn? _____

_____

_____

- Under what circumstances do you need to step outside of your comfort zone and exercise more courage? _____

_____

_____

- What holds you back from moving into your courage zone? _____

_____

_____

- How can you act more courageously? _____

_____

_____

Dive into Habit 3 by doing the following:

- Use a *planner* that will help you put first things first in your life.
- Review your *mission statement*. Think about what it means to you today. If you are not done with it, write the next draft.
- Make a *weekly plan*—remember to look at the big picture. Ask yourself if all of your big rocks are in place.
- *Plan daily*—with a weekly plan in place, you can focus on your daily priorities, tasks, and appointments.
- Make a list of your biggest *time wasters* and commit to focus your time on more important things.
- *Practice* daily a skill, talent, or habit you want to improve. Perhaps today it will be to practice being a better listener or to improve an athletic skill.
- This week in your planner or on a Notes page, *keep track* of all of the times you have done something that was important to you, although you didn't really want to do it at that particular moment.
- Review the baby steps on page 128.

PART III

The Public Victory™

The Stuff That Life Is Made Of

*"Keep in mind that the true measure of an individual is how
he treats a person who can do him absolutely no good."*
—Ann Landers

How would you define a Public Victory?

> Public Victory: Success with other people; your ability to get
> along with others.

1. Describe to someone how the Relationship Bank Account works and why it
   is important.

2. Make several copies of the Relationship Bank Account slip below. Give one to
   anyone who makes a deposit with you. This is like a thank-you note and will let
   the person know the value of the deposit he or she made with you.

Relationship Bank Account Deposit Slip

Date

Deposit

Amount   Signature

RELATIONSHIP BANK ACCOUNT

Refer to pp. 132-33.

Habit 4: Think Win-Win

Life Is an All-You-Can-Eat Buffet

> "Me lift thee and thee lift me, and we'll both ascend together."
> —John Greenleaf Whittier

Thinking win-win is the foundation for getting along well with other people.

Write your definition of win-win thinking. Once you have your description, share it with a friend. Use examples from your own life.

_____

_____

_____

_____

_____

Complete the following sentences.

It is hardest for me to think win-win when: _____

_____

_____

_____

_____

It is easiest for me to think win-win when: _____

_____

_____

_____

_____

When I practice win-win thinking, I enjoy the following benefits: _____

_____

_____

_____

_____

Refer to pp. 147–154.

Life Is an All-You-Can-Eat Buffet

What is win-lose?

> Win-Lose: When people only want to win and don't care if others lose.

Write about an experience where you had a win-lose mentality. How did you feel? Would you do things differently now? _____

_____

_____

_____

_____

_____

_____

_____

_____

_____

What is lose-win?

> Lose-Win: When people allow others to win even when it means they lose.

Write about an experience where you practiced lose-win or someone acted in a lose-win way toward you. How did you feel?

_____

_____

_____

_____

_____

_____

_____

_____

Habit 4: Think Win-Win

Life Is an All-You-Can-Eat Buffet

What is lose-lose?

> **Lose-Lose:** When people believe that if they go down, then others must go down with them.

List some lose-lose examples from history or current news events.

_____

_____

_____

_____

_____

_____

_____

_____

The following exercise will help you start living Habit 4.

List a specific situation that you may face in the next seven days that will require win-win thinking—it might be during a music lesson, at work, in a challenging class, or at home with your family. How will you prepare yourself to think win-win?

_____

_____

_____

_____

_____

_____

Later, record the experience as it actually happened. Write what the experience taught you about thinking win-win.

_____

_____

_____

_____

_____

Habit 5: Seek First to Understand, Then to Be Understood

You Have Two Ears and One Mouth...Hel-lo!

*"Before I can walk in another's shoes,
I must first remove my own."*
—Unknown

Habit 5: Seek First to Understand, Then to Be Understood means listen first, talk second; see things from another person's point of view before sharing your own.

When was the last time you tried walking in someone else's shoes? What was the experience like—actually trying to consider another person's point of view or idea before sharing yours?

Describe what happened and what you learned.

_____
_____
_____
_____
_____
_____
_____

Write your own definition of the following listening styles:

Spacing Out: _____
_____

Pretend Listening: _____
_____

Selective Listening: _____
_____

Word Listening: _____
_____

You Have Two Ears and One Mouth...Hel-lo!

Self-Centered Listening

Judging: _____

Advising: _____

Probing: _____

Genuine Listening: _____

Refer to pp. 168–171.

> Mirroring is repeating back in your own words what another person is saying and feeling. You don't judge or give advice.

Read the following statement.

"I feel so ugly. Nobody will ever ask me to the prom!"

A mirroring response could be:

"It sounds like you are discouraged about not being asked to the prom."

Now, try some of your own. Write a mirroring response for each of the following situations.

"No, you are not going out tonight!"

How would you respond using a mirroring response?

_____

_____

"You said I was the only one you wanted to be with, but that's not what I heard!"

How would you respond using a mirroring response?

_____

_____

Habit 5: Seek First to Understand, Then to Be Understood

You Have Two Ears and One Mouth...Hel-lo!

Then to Be Understood: This half of Habit 5 requires the courage to speak up.

When do you have the most difficult time giving feedback to others? Why?

_____

_____

_____

_____

_____

If you genuinely listen to another person, what happens when you then express your feelings, ideas, suggestions, or opinions?

_____

_____

_____

_____

_____

_____

When was the last time you kept your thoughts and feelings to yourself even though you really wanted to share them? Why didn't you share them? How did you feel about it?

_____

_____

_____

_____

_____

Now that you have analyzed your actions, what can you do to improve your practice of the second half of Habit 5, then to be understood?

_____

_____

_____

_____

_____

_____

The "High" Way

> "Differences challenge assumptions."
> —Anne Wilson Schaef

Synergy is when two or more people work together to create a better solution than either could alone.

To build and create synergy you have to look for it. You have to see that each individual is unique and value that uniqueness. Name some synergistic relationships in nature, in your school and in your home. For example, sequoia trees and the flight formation of geese both demonstrate synergistic relationships in nature.

_____

_____

_____

_____

_____

_____

_____

_____

_____

_____

The "High" Way

See how many different people you can learn about by completing the Synergy Boxes exercise. Write six more descriptions in the blank boxes below. Now, go and find people that match the descriptions and write their names in the appropriate box. See how many names you can write in each box during the next two days.

Synergy Boxes

Writes Stories, Plays, or Poetry		
	Speaks More Than One Language	An Excellent Athlete
Cooks Extremely Well		
Plays a Musical Instrument		Enjoys Studying Plants and Animals

Completing the Synergy Boxes exercise shows the importance of diversity and how each person is unique. But what about yourself? How are you different from others?

_____

_____

_____

_____

Refer to pp. 183–184.

Habit 6: Synergize
The "High" Way

Think through the following questions carefully before answering them.

1. Some people love to be with groups of people. Some people like to spend much of their time alone. How do you prefer to spend your time? Why?

_____

_____

_____

2. Some people are dreamers; they're always thinking of new possibilities, new ways of doing things. Some people are very practical; they like to study the world and know how to do things. Which type of person are you? Why?

_____

_____

_____

3. Some people make decisions based on their feelings and how they think others might feel. Other people make decisions based on facts. How do you prefer to make decisions? Why?

_____

_____

_____

4. Some people like their lives planned out and scheduled. Other people like to be surprised or just see what happens. Which way do you prefer? Why?

_____

_____

_____

Created by the Alabama Cooperative Extension System at Auburn University.

The "High" Way

> The "high" way is finding a better solution than win-lose, lose-win, or lose-lose, and it always produces more.

1. Write down an important issue that you, your community, your school, or your family is facing right now. Maybe it's violence at school, a dress code, or a community issue, such as changing the curfew for teenagers.

Issue/Problem

_____

_____

_____

_____

_____

_____

2. Organize a group of four or more people to discuss the issue you chose. Individually, think of ways to improve or change the problem.

3. On the following page, fill in the bubbles with the different solutions each of you come up with.

4. Use your imagination as you brainstorm new ideas.

5. Together, decide which solution will make the biggest difference. Write your group's idea in the solution box. Be sure to use the habit of synergy.

The "High" Way

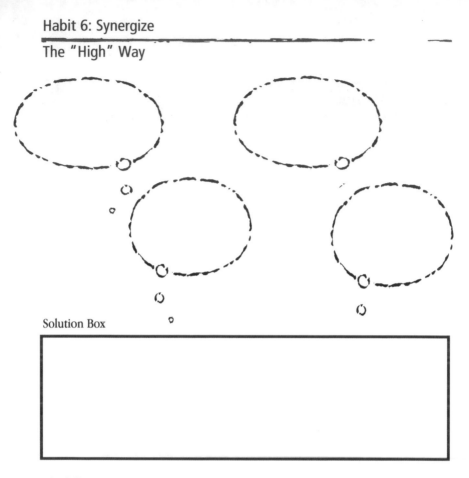

Solution Box

The following activities will help you dive into Habit 6: Synergize. Choose two of them to complete.

- Find a safe international pen-pal club on the Internet and submit your name. This will allow you to get to know people from different cultures and backgrounds.
- Invite someone from a different cultural background to lunch. Ask about his or her country and unique customs.
- Before you turn in your next class writing assignment or project, ask a friend to review it and make suggestions. Be prepared to make changes based on the new insights you receive.
- Record any of the above experiences in your journal or on a Notes page. Write what you learned about synergy.
- Review the baby steps on p. 202.

Refer to p. 195.

PART IV

Renewal

It's "Me Time"

"To keep a lamp burning, we have to keep putting oil in it."
—Mother Teresa

> Habit 7: Sharpen the Saw is about renewing yourself and balancing the key areas of your life: physical, mental, social/emotional, and spiritual.

Set a timer or alarm for three minutes. Then, in the boxes below, list all of the things you want to do to sharpen your saw in each of the four categories.

BODY (physical)	HEART (relationships)
SOUL (spiritual)	BRAIN (mental)

Habit 7: Sharpen the Saw

It's "Me Time"

Here's a plan to help you sharpen your saw physically. Answer each of the questions listed below, then your plan will be set and waiting for you to take action.

What physical activities do you like to do? Are there any activities you haven't tried, but would like to? Make a list.

Like to Do	Want to Try

Choose a few items on your list and write them in the spaces under "Activity" on the chart below. Decide when, where, and how you will do these activities. Also write how long you'll spend doing each activity. Don't forget to involve people who can participate with you or encourage you to sharpen your saw physically.

ACTIVITY	WHEN, WHERE, HOW	LENGTH OF TIME
running	Monday and Wednesday in the park with Nina	25 minutes

Make a copy of the chart above and place it somewhere you will see it daily or record the information in your planner.

Refer to p. 208.

Sharpening the saw physically is not limited just to physical exercise. Think about the food you eat. Here's a plan to help you sharpen your saw regarding nutrition. Answer each of the following questions, then your plan will be set and waiting for you to take action.

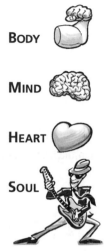

BODY

MIND

HEART

SOUL

What foods did you eat last weekend that were not healthy for your body?

_____
_____
_____
_____

How can you change your eating habits?

_____
_____
_____
_____

Now, create a plan that will help you focus on good nutritional habits.

_____
_____
_____
_____

Refer to p. 209.

Habit 7: Sharpen the Saw

It's "Me Time"

MIND To care for your brain is to sharpen the saw mentally. Make a list of skills or talents you enjoy or might like to learn.

- Chess
-
-
-
-
-

What new skill can you commit to learn in the next month? _____

Here is another activity to keep your brain sharp:

Interview someone you admire and would like to know more about. Ask about his or her life, challenges, successes, history, and interests. Make your own list of questions below.

Below is an example to get you started:

- What made you decide to become a...?
-
-
-
-
-

What did you learn from this interview?

_____

_____

_____

_____

Refer to p. 218.

HEART Caring for your heart is how you sharpen the saw socially and emotionally. Look at it as a Relationship Bank Account. Care for your heart by making deposits. Add your own ideas of deposits to the list below. Be specific.

• Write a thank-you note to _____.

•

•

•

•

•

Answer the following questions:

Which of your relationships are the most important?

_____

_____

Are you making deposits into these relationships? What are you doing?

_____

_____

How can you improve your most important relationships?

_____

_____

To boost your emotional well-being, why not start your own humor corner today? Write your favorite joke below or paste in a cartoon, then share it with someone.

Refer to p. 233.

Habit 7: Sharpen the Saw

It's "Me Time"

Soul

Caring for your soul is how you sharpen the saw spiritually. The following activities will help you do this.
- Meditate
- Volunteer to read to a child for an hour
- Listen to inspiring music

What other activities do you enjoy that will help awaken your soul? List them below.

-
-
-
-
-

Select one or two items from the lists above and set up a plan to sharpen your saw spiritually. Be sure to think about people that can participate with you or encourage you to sharpen your saw.

ACTIVITY	WHEN, WHERE, HOW	LENGTH OF TIME
Read to a child	Thursdays, after school, at the hospital	1 hour

Make a copy of the commitments you have made to sharpen your saw spiritually and place it somewhere you will see it daily. Your planner would be an excellent place to record these goals.

Refer to pp. 234–235.

Kid, You'll Move Mountains

"If you do not hope, you will not find what is beyond your hopes."
—St. Clement of Alexandria

You've reached the last pages of this workbook! Now, return to p. 2 of this workbook and review the personal expectations you wrote down.

Did you meet your expectations? If you feel you didn't, what do you need to do now?

_____

_____

_____

_____

_____

_____

_____

_____

_____

What valuable things did you learn that you didn't expect to learn?

_____

_____

_____

_____

_____

_____

_____

_____

_____

Kid, You'll Move Mountains

How will you apply the 7 Habits in the next week? month? year?

_____

_____

_____

_____

_____

_____

_____

Did you share what you learned? How did it make a difference?

_____

_____

_____

_____

_____

_____

_____

How will you continue to share what you've learned from the 7 Habits?

_____

_____

_____

_____

_____

_____

_____

Other insights:

_____

_____

_____

_____

_____

_____

_____

Notes

Notes

Notes

Notes

Notes

Notes